LifeCaps P

The Red Priest

The Life of Antonio Vivaldi

By James Fritz

BOOKCAPS

BookCaps™ Study Guides

www.bookcaps.com

Table of Contents

ABOUT LIFECAPS 3

INTRODUCTION 4

CHAPTER 1: CHILDHOOD AND EDUCATION 6

CHAPTER 2: HOSPITAL OF MERCY...17

CHAPTER 3: OPERA IMPRESARIO...35

CHAPTER 4: MANTUA AND THE FOUR SEASONS....................59

    A ROYAL APPOINTMENT 60
    THE FOUR SEASONS 75

CHAPTER 5: LATER LIFE 78

CHAPTER 6: CONCLUSION AND LEGACY................................92

BIBLIOGRAPHY..99

About LifeCaps

LifeCaps is an imprint of BookCaps™ Study Guides. With each book, a lesser known or sometimes forgotten life is recapped. We publish a wide array of topics (from baseball and music to literature and philosophy), so check our growing catalogue regularly (**www.bookcaps.com**) to see our newest books.

Introduction

Born in Venice, Italy, Antonio Vivaldi was one of
the most influential and highly regarded Baroque
composers, although his fame blazed only
briefly. He is most remembered for his
concertos, particularly "The Four Seasons," but
his overall production was enormous, ranging
from orchestral and vocal music for both secular
and church settings, as well as opera scores and
libretti. In addition, Vivaldi was a master violinist
and spent much of his career as an instructor at
a famous institution for girls, the Hospital of
Mercy. He was educated as a priest, but poor
health and probably a lack of interest in the
calling encouraged him to follow another path in
life.

During his lifetime, the red-haired virtuoso and opera impresario was easily among the most famous musicians in Italy; this fame eventually extended throughout civilized Europe. His name was sufficient to open doors to the richest and most powerful people in the Western world. Before his death, however, his heyday had long passed. After an extended period of obscurity, the music of Vivaldi underwent a revival in the early 20th century.

Chapter 1: Childhood and Education

Antonio Lucio Vivaldi, son of Giovanni Battista Vivaldi and Camilla Calicchio, was born in the Castello district of Venice, Italy on March 4, 1678. At that time, Venice was the capital of an independent republic of the same name, also known as the "Most Serene Republic." He was immediately baptized at home, a somewhat unusual practice; his church baptism did not take place until May 6, 1678 at St. Giovanni's. Possible reasons for the hasty ceremony may have been an earthquake earlier in the day, the infant's poor health, or both. He may even have been a few weeks premature. In addition to the home baptism, it's possible that Vivaldi's mother may have promised her son to the priesthood as a token of gratitude for surviving the earthquake.

Vivaldi was born into a relatively poor but not unaccomplished family. His parents were married the year before his birth, in August 1677. Vivaldi's father had started on a career as a barber prior to becoming a professional violinist. Giovanni Battista taught his son everything who knew about playing the violin, both theoretical and practical. In 1685, he cofounded a highly regarded musical fraternity known as the Sovvegno Dei Musicisti di Santa Cecilia. The director of the group, Giovanni Legrenzi, was an already famous figure in the Venetian music scene. As a father and son pair, the Vivaldis traveled around Venice giving virtuoso performances. At some point, perhaps quite early on, the son surpassed the father in technical prowess. However, Antonio Vivaldi was not a child prodigy in the same sense as Mozart; his talents were painstakingly developed through rigorous study and practice.

Eight other children were born to Giovanni and Camilla. Little more than their names is known with certainty: Margarita Gabriela, Cecilia Maria, Bonaventura Tomaso, Zanetta Anna, Antonia Lucio, Francesco Gaetano, Iseppo Santo and Guiseppe. Francesco may have followed in his father's footsteps in becoming a moderately successful barber and wigmaker, but he found himself on the wrong side of the law after insulting a nobleman. Another brother, Iseppo, was exiled from Venice for at least three years after a street fight. None of the other Vivaldi children achieved lasting fame, and none pursued music as a serious calling. Red hair was a common identifiable trait among the family, passed down from Giovanni, with Antonio later earning the memorable nickname "The Red Priest."

In the late 17th and early 18th century, Venice was a city in decline geopolitically, but still a powerhouse culturally. Indeed, Venice was an art and music mecca for European tourists from as far away as London, Paris and Hamburg, most of them among the wealthy and noble. The city excelled particularly in the production of both sacred and popular music. Giovanni Legrenzi, for instance, was known as an innovator and trend setter; he dramatically reorganized and enlarged the orchestra at St. Mark's church. In 1685, he employed Vivaldi's father as a violinist in the orchestra. He earned an annual salary of 15 ducats.

By virtue of having an exceptionally talented violinist as a father, as well as growing up in the musical capital of Europe, young Antonio Vivaldi had the opportunity to learn from the most talented musicians of his generation. Giovanni Battista was his son's first and possibly only serious violin instructor; he also took him to the premier musical venues in the city, including, churches, opera houses and conservatories. A visitor's guide to Venice from 1706 listed both the elder and junior Vivaldis as leading violin masters. Vivaldi may have experimented with the harpsichord as well, but he never became a true master of the instrument. Giovanni Legrenzi, his father's employer and conductor at St. Mark's, may also have been an early teacher, but this is not proven. A short piece of music dated to 1691 and attributed to Vivaldi shows a distinct Legrenzi influence. Because Legrenzi died when the young virtuoso was only 12, however, his influence could not have been too great. There is also evidence that Vivaldi may have occasionally played at St. Mark's as a substitute musician or perhaps just an assistant. Upon taking religious orders at 15, he would have probably been his own instructor, building upon the foundation laid by his father.

Despite being immersed in music almost from birth, Vivaldi may not at first have seen musicianship as a career path. Financial stress within the family may have forced the young man to choose a more practical alternative. As such, he officially began his church education in September 1693. The only requirements for acceptance into the priesthood were proof of birth and baptism and two witnesses attesting to the applicant's moral character. The fact that he entered the priesthood as the eldest son betrayed the family's social class; in more well-to-do families, usually only the youngest son would don the robes, trusting in the charity of parents and older siblings to support them if need be. It was three years before Vivaldi completed the minor orders, becoming an acolyte in 1696. He became a subdeacon in 1699, and then a deacon in 1700. The priesthood, as a profession, was a common enough choice for young men in the 17th century, much more so than today. By one estimate, about 1 in 20 men were employed by the church in one capacity or another. For Vivaldi and his family, the priesthood may have offered a means to earn a free, quality education, as well as a measure of social respectability.

Vivaldi's priestly education did not include living in a traditional seminary. Instead, he was apprenticed to a senior priest at St. Germiniano. He later took instruction from another church leader at San Giovanni; both churches were near St. Mark's in Venice, not far from Vivaldi's place of birth. Neither his religious nor his musical education took him away from home. He did not leave Venice for any extended period until well into adulthood. During his near-decade of apprenticeship, there was only one reference to any musical performance. At the St. Mark's Christmas concert in 1696, Vivaldi was listed as a violinist.

The training required to become a full priest was arduous, but especially so for Vivaldi. He needed almost ten years to graduate, not earning his place in the priesthood until March 23, 1703. His slow progress may have been the result of poor health. In letters to colleagues, Vivaldi complained of tightness in his chest that had plagued him since birth. He had trouble walking far or going up steps, especially after certain meals. Asthma has been identified as the likely source of his symptoms. Either way, his frail health meant that the responsibilities of priesthood, particularly saying daily Mass, were too much for him. He led his last official service only a year after putting on the priestly robes, turning his full attention to the composition of music. According to one story, which has nothing substantial to support it other than being a romantic idea, Vivaldi would leave Mass unfinished, not because of shortness of breath, but because a particularly remarkable musical theme struck his imagination, and he had to quickly write it down.

Even while diligently studying as an apprentice, Vivaldi did not abandon his musical inclinations. In fact, there is evidence that he gave as much time and energy to music theory and practice during his education as he did to the rules and procedures of being a priest. At the time, it was not uncommon for members of the priesthood to have "dual careers"—alternating church responsibilities with artistic endeavors, science or politics. The elite level of musicianship that Vivaldi had achieved by 1703, when he officially became a priest, shows that he had not only maintained his practice regimen, but sought to expand his powers even further.

Chapter 2: Hospital of Mercy

Antonio Vivaldi's first professional musical appointment was as Master of Violin at the Hospital of Mercy in 1703. His initial salary was 60 ducats a year, four times what his father was earning at St. Mark's. In modern terminology, the Hospital of Mercy was more like an orphanage or foster home, so called only because it was physically attached to a medical an institution. It was one of four such establishments in Venice that had built sterling reputations as schools of music and music instruction. These included the Beggars' Hospital, Hospital of the Incurables, and the Small Hospital, in addition to the Hospital of Mercy. These particular institutions only accepted girls. Male instructors were frequently selected from the priesthood, for obvious reasons.

The Venetian hospitals occupied a weighty position in the European musical scene, as well as the history of music in general. Originally, the institutions were strictly intended as charitable services for abandoned or orphaned children. Basic and religious education were standard fare at all hospitals, but music also played a role from the very beginning. A combination of government and private funds helped ensure that every girl received room, board and adequate instruction. The hospitals' reputation for turning out masterful instrumentalists steadily grew, in turn changing the focus of the hospitals to something more commercial. As a mecca for rich and cultured tourists, there was a fortune to be made from high caliber musical performances. Eventually, they accepted not only orphans, but daughters of wealthy families who wanted the best possible musical instruction. Some especially talented girls stayed at the hospitals until middle age, leading the next generation and acquiring international fame for themselves.

Hospitals were among the three main institutions of music in Venice by the time Vivaldi took his post as Master of Violin. The opera houses and churches were the other two. Each catered to a different audience and a different sensibility. The church once occupied the top rung of the ladder, but by the 18th century, the hospitals had supplanted them. Only the truly accomplished geniuses, of which Vivaldi was certainly one, managed to cross over and achieve success in each of these venues. Music was woven into the fabric of Venetian life like no other cultural institution. It has been compared to a combination of television, theater and professional sports—none of which then existed, of course. During Carnival, an annual winter celebration revolving around Christmas, the opera houses would fill with crowds every day and night, representing every social class in Venice. Throughout the year, Saturdays, Sundays and holidays were all punctuated with various musical performances.

Before Vivaldi's appointment at the Hospital of Mercy, some of the governors and leading masters expressed an interest in raising their institution's already high standards. An expansion and reorganization of the orchestra was enacted, bringing in new instruments and making possible cutting-edge arrangements. As such, there were empty positions to be filled, including Masters of Violin Viola. Nothing remains of Vivaldi's application process, but it's likely that his reputation preceded him. He was given the official title of Master of Violin, but he also had responsibility over the viola players. His main duty was technical instruction in each instrument and instruction in music theory. Supplemental duties included acquiring new instruments and parts as necessary, playing in or directing the orchestra when other Masters were absent, and composing new works for the Hospital for specific occasions.

Despite effectively leaving the priesthood behind, the governors at the Hospital of Mercy expected Vivaldi to also lead Mass, seeing as he had the formal training to do so. He was reportedly contracted at 80 ducats a year for daily Mass but was paid somewhat less than this. His ever-present health complaints meant that he simply couldn't give the service every day. However, never did his condition seem to interfere with his music performance or instruction, which has caused some historians to wonder how much of Vivaldi's health problems were real and how much were faked in order to avoid burdensome tasks.

Any Venetian composer or instrumentalist worth his salt eventually held a position at one of the hospitals, if only temporarily. An instructorship meant not only a competitive and dependable salary, but also freedom and prestige. While playing violin at St. Mark's, Giovanni Battista, Vivaldi's father, also held a post as Master of Instruments at the Beggars' Hospital. Typically, boards of governors managed the hiring and firing of music instructors. At the Hospital of Mercy, each appointed instructor was put to an annual vote to determine their status. Two-thirds majority was required to retain a position.

In 1705, Vivaldi published his first official sheet music—a set of trio sonatas dedicated to Count Annibale Gambara. Trio sonatas were all the rage at the time, though concertos and solo sonatas were gaining traction. The lengthy dedication is thoroughly in keeping with the style expected in first publications. Vivaldi apologized for his mediocre skills and begged the nobleman's protection against harsh and heartless critics. Ideally, a compelling dedication would earn the composer a financial kickback and perhaps even a lifelong patron.

Though his first few years at the Hospital of Mercy were certainly productive, they were not without friction. The annual vote on whether to retain his services was often hotly contested. In 1707, he received six votes in favor to three against; two years later and the vote was seven to six. When a former supporter crossed the aisle, Vivaldi was officially out as Master of Violin. Reports suggested that the "Red Priest's" independent personality, coupled with his clearly high ambitions, made for a tense relationship at best with the board of governors. Though perhaps devastating at the time, Vivaldi's ouster did have one beneficial outcome: the governors quickly realized just how valuable the Master of Violin had made himself during his six-year tenure. By 1711, he was reappointed to his former position.

During the two-year interval when he was no longer associated with the Hospital of Mercy, Vivaldi likely made his first steps toward a long-term relationship with the opera. He contributed time and energy, as well as some of his own money, to the success of the San Angelo Theatre, an opera house that had fallen on hard times. The previous impresario, or managing director, had nearly bankrupted the establishment after a series of poor business decisions. Vivaldi took seized the moment, composing music for a popular audience for the first time; the hiatus from his duties as Master of Violin for the Hospital of Mercy was, therefore, a fantastic opportunity to expand his creative horizons. Of course, not all of his activities between 1709 and 1711 can be easily accounted for; some sources indicate that he traveled outside of Venice in search of gainful employment.

With Vivaldi's reappointment as Master of Violin, he returned to a state of relative financial stability, but he never quite gave up his musical ramblings. After 1711, he no longer taught viola, nor did he oversee religious services. He published a noteworthy instrumental work, "The Harmonic Inspiration," which demonstrated his aptitude for the concerto, the newly resurgent genre of the day. In hindsight, "The Harmonic Inspiration" was among the most important collections of music produced in the 18th century. Its influence spread across the entire continent, providing a new direction for an entire generation of instrumental musicians. People even began referring to the "Vivaldian method" of composition.

In 1713, a shakeup at the hospital meant more changes for Vivaldi and some tough decisions for the board of governors. Choral Master Francesco Gasparini had requested and been granted a sick leave, but this turned out to be a ruse. Gasparini had no intention of returning to his post. He moved to Florence and then Rome, never setting foot in Venice again. The Hospital of Mercy was left with a vacancy at one of its most prominent positions of authority.

The essential responsibility of the Choral Master was to write lyrics and compose music to accompany vocal ensembles. For a time, the other masters chipped in and more or less filled the void, but it was a balancing act. It soon became clear that Vivaldi was the most gifted among the staff. Thus, most of the Choral Master's duties ultimately fell upon him. The governors recognized the extra work that their Master of Violin was giving them; at a meeting, the board approved a one-time payment of 50 ducats in recognition of Vivaldi's exceptional efforts. He either was not offered or did seek a more permanent, official status as Choral Master. Another factor working against him was his increasing visibility as an opera composer and impresario. This somewhat "low brow" calling was probably seen to be unsuitable for a Choral Master at a celebrated institution such as the Hospital of Mercy. At any rate, Vivaldi was the de facto Choral Master until the appointment of Carlo Luigi Pietragrua in 1719. Other vacancy periods in 1726 and 1737 to 1739 were likely filled in by the Master of Violin.

Although he was sometimes difficult to manage and had many outside interests competing for his attention, the Hospital of Mercy's reputation as a cultural landmark of the first order was enhanced by having Antonio Vivaldi on its staff. Understanding this, the governors were willing to give their Master of Violin some leverage. In May 1713, he was granted a one-month leave to arrange for the premier of his new opera. *Ottone in Villa* opened at the Grazie Theatre in Vicenza, across the channel from Venice.

Vivaldi's living arrangements and personal details are difficult to pick out from the few official documents and letters that have survived to the present day. Nothing is known of his extended family. He rented a house near St. Mark's Square from 1705 to 1708, but it's unknown whether he was alone or lived with family members or housemates. From 1711 to 1722, Vivaldi and his father rented an apartment even closer to St. Mark's for 42 ducats a year. For a brief time, he also rented a small dwelling adjacent to San Angelo Theatre, possibly to be even closer to his work and keep an eye on his business interests.

With the publication of "The Harmonic Inspiration," Vivaldi's international reputation was firmly established. Visiting nobles and musicians sought out the violin virtuoso; a brief history of one such encounter actually survives. In 1715, German nobleman Johann Friedrich Armand von Uffenbach was in Venice during the winter Carnival. He attended San Angelo Theatre four times in a few weeks just to see Vivaldi's arrangement of a well-known opera. In between acts, the musician himself walked on stage and treated the audience to a virtuoso solo performance. Uffenbach was entranced and requested a meeting. He commissioned Vivaldi to write some unique, personalized music for him, paying him up front. An amateur instrumentalist himself, he also paid Vivaldi for the privilege of a series of private lessons based on the new compositions. No doubt there were similar instances of wealthy tourists bestowing their affection and their money on the "Red Priest."

In summary, the period from 1703 to about 1713 was a transitional decade for Vivaldi. He left the priesthood behind and took a position teaching young girls the intricacies of the violin. His talent was increasingly recognized by both locals and the elites in Italy, Germany and France. After a dismissal from his post as Master of Violin, Vivaldi stretched his wings, discovering enormous potential in the most democratic of Baroque musical genres: opera.

Chapter 3: Opera Impresario

Italy was the birthplace of modern opera. Given its musical reputation, it's no surprise that Venice was home to the first public opera house, or theatre. In 1637, the opera *Andromeda* was performed in front of a captivated audience. With the genie out of the bottle, the growth and experimentation in Venetian opera continued at a rapid pace for the next several decades. By the end of the 17th century, there were approximately 18 theatres within the city. Despite this obvious success, running an opera house was still a risky business proposition.

Among the rich, it was considered fashionable to have a stake in an opera house. Usually, landowners would sign off on the use of their land for the purposes of building just such an establishment. In this way, the wealthy took on little of the actual risk. These investors were also given free or nearly free seats at any establishment in the city. Cash flow, therefore, became a serious issue, not only because the elite clientele often paid nothing for admittance.

Actors and actresses represented another drain on theatre resources. These singing masters demanded absurdly high fees, along with unusual stipulations regarding dress and scenery. They often inserted songs of their own choosing into the arrangement, probably leading to confusion for the audience. Most operas were performed only once or twice, highlighting the need for composers to work hastily.

Furthermore, operas were usually only stage during three short seasons: Carnival (winter), spring and fall. The analogy has been made that opera in Venice was the equivalent of television—not high art, exactly, but more like a bright, noisy distraction for the general public.

The design of 17th century Venetian opera houses was generally similar from one to the next. Along both sides were several floors of luxury boxes. These were usually the only places within the theatre with actual seats. Boxes were rented out for whole seasons or indefinitely. Each box had shades that could be drawn down if the guests wanted to do something else—eat or play cards, for example. In the middle was an open area for the "rabble," who like the wealthy nobles sitting above them, often paid little or nothing for the privilege of seeing and hearing the latest production. It was typical, not just in Italy, for the box seat clients to throw trash and spit on the patrons below. The stage itself varied in its level of sophistication. Some had elaborate machinery, making swift and frequent set changes possible. Others were poorly lit and simplistic, forcing audiences to use their imagination.

An opera impresario in 18th century Venice was a combination of executive producer and artistic director. He was responsible for both artistic decisions, such as costumes and set design, and talent scouting. Most importantly, the impresario absorbed all the risks involved in a new production; performers and production assistant earned their fees regardless of ticket sales. For the man in charge of everything, however, one lousy show could lead to bankruptcy. On the other hand, a successful show could earn a healthy profit for the impresario, helping him create a reputation for excellent entertainment. While an opera typically had one or more composers and lyricists, the impresario ensured that everything came together in a seamless whole.

Vivaldi's involvement with the Venetian stage almost certainly predates his first opera. His father often played in the orchestra of local opera houses. Even fellow instructors at the Hospital of Mercy had ties to theatre. Gasparini, the Choral Master who left in 1713, had for many years been a regular produce of popular operas. Francesco Saturini was a neighbor and the impresario of San Angelo, as well as perhaps being a shadowy underworld figure. Vivaldi also included renowned performers among his acquaintances, such as the tenor Paita. Apart from personal contacts, there was already a strong intersection of sacred and popular music in Venice. Instrumentalists and vocalists often performed year-round with churches and earned supplemental income during the short opera seasons. In short, it would not have been difficult for the Master of Violin to segue into an opera career if the urge took him.

The urge did indeed take Vivaldi sometime between 1709 and 1711. Relieved of his responsibilities at the Hospital of Mercy, he realized that opera represented a perfectly acceptable way to expand on his musical ideas. Vivaldi had a take-charge personality (possibly one of the reasons for friction with Hospital governors), and the position of impresario would have appealed to him. Not only that, success in opera represented a chance to supplement his modest income.

Vivaldi's first opera, *Ottone in villa*, was an unqualified success. It was revived at least twice, in 1715 and 1729. It's possible that he chose Vicenza as the location for his debut rather than his hometown out of fear of failure: Vivaldi was notoriously sensitive to criticism. He collaborated on the libretto—the written text of the opera, including stage directions—with Domenico Lalli, who was on the run from the authorities in another part of Italy and was using a fake name. They worked together several more times, with Lalli apparently bright enough to avoid capture.

After the success of *Ottone in villa*, Vivaldi turned his attention to Venice. Specifically, he had his eyes set on the San Angelo Theatre, located directly on the Grand Canal. The impresario, Saturini, was a personal acquaintance. The full story behind San Angelo is twisted and strange. Originally, the Capello and Marcello families had given Saturini the right to use their property to construct and manage a new theatre. This was 1676, two years before Vivaldi's birth. At the end of an agreed-upon term, Saturini was supposed to turn the facility back over to the landowners. Instead, he sued them, as well as all the wealthy patrons who owned money to the theatre. Somehow, he came out from the legal maneuvers unscathed and still in control of San Angelo. These backroom dealings seem to have caught up with him by 1713, when he requested Vivaldi to come in and take over some aspects of management. The Master of Violin readily agreed. He scouted talent for San Angelo Theatre off and on for the rest of his opera career, which lasted until at least 1739.

San Angelo was a middle-of-the-road theatre in Venice, but its profile was certainly lifted with the help of Vivaldi. The impresario could not afford the kind of set designs or singing talents of the leading opera houses, such as San Giovanni Grisostomo or San Cassiano, so he had to compensate with extraordinary musical scores and librettos. For the most part, Vivaldi was successful. Between 1714 and 1739, he premiered at least 18 operas at San Angelo.

Shortly after the Vicenzan premiere, Vivaldi produced *Orlando finto pazzo* in the fall season of 1714. It was his first Venetian opera, but he did not limit himself to his hometown. During the same season, he also produced a highly successful revival of *Orlando furioso*, one of the first great operas. Soon, he was providing his services for another show in Vicenza, *Rodomonte sdegnato*. During the course of the next 25 years, his work as impresario took him well outside his home region. His name is listed prominently on opera programs in cities like Rome, Florence, Mantua and Milan. In all likelihood, his reach extended beyond these culturally rich cities—probably even beyond Italy.

As impresario, Vivaldi was often forced into the position of hastily composing vocal and instrumental music for the operas he was producing. Since operas did not run for more than one or two shows, the public was constantly expecting new entertainment, or at least imaginative revivals of older performances. Impresarios often had to be creative to satisfy this demand. In the case of Vivaldi, he sometimes wrote vocal and instrumental accompaniments that followed identical structures, which saved time but lead to uninspiring music for such a master composer. On one sheet where he was writing just such a score, he scribbled angrily and expressed his view that he was doing hack work. Still, Vivaldi had a reputation for being a rapid composer whose productions did not falter in quality even when he was rushed. The meeting with Uffenbach was a prime example; he reportedly wrote 10 original instrumental pieces for the visiting German in only 3 days.

Opera production also required a bit of recycling from time to time. Popular arias were often plucked from earlier shows and inserted into new scores, with not too much thought on whether the addition made sense. The actors and actresses themselves did nothing to help advance the plot, either. Acting was, in fact, a non-factor; performers gave all their attention to singing technique, walking around the stage or unbuttoning costumes as they saw fit. In a sense, familiarity was expected. A highly successful opera could lay the foundation for countless "spinoffs." Such was the case with Vivaldi's best work.

For the Carnival of 1715/1716, Vivaldi composed one of his most enduring operas. *La costanza trionfante de gl'amori e de gl'odii* opened at the San Moise Theatre in Venice. Although he was officially impresario at San Angelo, he was not contractually bound there; it's uncertain how much responsibility he had to the theatre owners at San Moise. A bona fide success, *La costanza* was reworked at least twice: in 1718, Vivaldi produced *Artabano*; another major revision of the source material was introduced in 1732 with *Doriclea*. Each adapted version of *La costanza* was greeted with fanfare and earned healthy returns for Vivaldi. Some parts of the opera continued to be "borrowed" and worked into new productions even after the impresario's retirement and death.

The spring of 1716 introduced Vivaldi to a fellow violin virtuoso who would be hugely important in preserving his legacy, though neither of them knew it at the time. Johann Georg Pisendel arrived from Dresden, Germany in 1716. He quickly befriended Vivaldi, taking lessons from the Italian master. Pisendel collected as many music manuscripts as possible, mostly those of Vivaldi, for his return home. Once back in Dresden, he became leader of the court orchestra. From this position of influence, Pisendel helped create the German "Vivaldi cult," ensuring the continuance of the Vivaldian style for generations to come.

In the fall of 1716, Vivaldi reunited with his former collaborator, Dominic Lalli. They produced *Arsilda regina di Ponto*, another rousing success. The pairing produced some of Vivaldi's best operas, but legal trouble for Lalli forced him to keep a low profile much of the time.

Vivaldi produced one of his most highly regarded opera scores for the Carnival in 1716/1717. *L'incoronazione di Dario* premiered in January at the San Angelo Theatre. Unfortunately, though the score was considered among his best, the libretto was universally panned. The libretto was, in fact, recycled from a previous opera with little time for revision. Considering that most audiences only half paid attention to the productions anyway, a subpar libretto did not seem to harm Vivaldi's status.

The period from about 1713 to 1718 was one of enormous energy and productivity for Vivaldi. It's easy to forget that, in addition to producing one or more operas each season, he was also publishing original instrumental music and continuing to teach violin at the Hospital of Mercy. Perhaps his being spread so thin explains why the board of governors ousted him briefly in 1716. By way of an apology, Vivaldi wrote *Juditha triumphans*, a "sacred military oratorio" in honor of Venetian soldiers fighting against Ottoman invaders. Overall, however, job insecurity at the hospital no doubt encouraged him to redouble his efforts as impresario.

By 1718, Vivaldi began actively casting his net wider than his hometown. Between 1718 and 1725, only 2 of his operas were produced and performed in Venice. His reputation for excellence had reached the point that he was receiving numerous offers of employment from neighboring cities, even foreign nations. In the spring of 1718, he accepted one of these lucrative offers and became court music director for the Prince of Hesse-Darmstadt in Mantua. Despite his royal appointment, Vivaldi's work in the opera did not noticeably slow down.

In Mantua, Vivaldi quickly established himself as a force to be reckoned with on the opera scene. In his two years' residence in the city, he composed three new operas. Writing near the end of his career in 1739, the violin master and opera impresario claimed to have been responsible for 94 operas. How many of these were wholly original and how many were reworkings or revivals is impossible to say. If the number he stated was correct, then half of his operas were lost to history.

Vivaldi returned to his hometown in 1720, but he did not immediately resume his work at the San Angelo Theatre. A satirical pamphlet that was releases the same year—"The Fashionable Theatre"—poked fun at Venetian opera in general, but Vivaldi in particular. He was caricatured on the front as an angel tapping his feet and playing violin. It was speculated that the theatre's property owners, the Cappello and Marcello families, were behind the scandalous publication. At any rate, Vivaldi seemed to deliberately avoid his old stomping grounds, whether because of "The Fashionable Theatre" or for some other reason is unknown. He did not produce another opera for San Angelo until 1725.

In 1724, Vivaldi singlehandedly revitalized opera with his introduction of the "Lombard" style. With the debut of *pasticcio La virtu trionfante* in Rome, audiences and critics agreed that the new musical rhythm was superior to anything that had come before it. One writer noted that opera patrons ignored any new productions that did not adopt the Lombard style. Vivaldi may not have invented the new form, but he was undeniably responsible for making it popular throughout Italy.

Vivaldi finally returned to his former position as impresario of San Angelo in 1726. Between 1725 and 1728, he produced an astonishing 7 new operas for the theatre, and at least 4 for other venues. Vivaldi may have even rescued Florence's famed Pergola Theatre from ruin in 1727; his staging of *Ipermestra* not only turned the theatre's finances around, it made a gondola-load of money for the impresario.

The passage of three centuries has left few clues as to Vivaldi's personal life, but the year 1726 is a minor exception. It was then that Anna Giro made her first appearance on Vivaldi's stage in *Dorilla*. The young actress was neither especially beautiful nor a gifted singer, but she was noted for her acting ability and a certain kind of personal magnetism. She, maybe only 16 at the time, became fast friends with the much older Vivaldi, who took her on as a kind of protégé. Naturally, rumors soon flew around the pair like biting flies. Vivaldi strongly denied any wrongdoing, and there's no evidence that there relationship was anything more than an honest friendship. In his frequent travels around Italy and Europe, Vivaldi often brought along Giro and her sisters as nurses and companions, adding to the whispers of gossip mongers.

Outside of the cultural centers of Italy—Venice, Florence, Rome—Germany was the largest consumer of Vivaldi's operatic works. Unfortunately, this adoration did not translate into much income for the impresario. He had only a single patron, Count Franz Anton Sporck, who paid him a commission for the use of his art. As a wealthy music lover, Count Sporck had a noticeable influence on the direction of taste and fashion. He promoted Vivaldi in Prague, just as years later he promoted Johann Sebastian Bach. In 18th century Europe, these kinds of social networks and affiliations were necessary to achieve anything more than local, temporary recognition. Vivaldi was an expert at self-promotion and politicking, though his music always came first.

Generally, the 1730s consisted of a gradual distancing between Vivaldi and San Angelo Theatre. Carnival 1732 saw Vivaldi producing operas in both Mantua and Verona. At various times, he was officially listed as an impresario in Pavia (1731), Mantua (1732), Verona (1735), Treviso (1737) and Ancona (1738). The year 1736 was especially productive and was likely his last great burst of original, trendsetting work. In a single year, he created four entirely new operas: *Adelaide, Griselda, Aristide* and *Ginerva*. *Aristide* was Vivaldi's first and only musical comedy. On November 7, 1739, *Faraspe* was produced at San Angelo. It was not only the celebrated impresario's last work for the theatre, it was also his last known operatic work, period.

Chapter 4: Mantua and the Four Seasons

A Royal Appointment

A relatively short distance from Venice and Vicenza, in the Lombardy region of Italy, lies the former republic of Mantua. In Antonio Vivaldi's time, Mantua was actually a possession of Austria, or more accurately, the Habsburg Empire. During the Spanish War of Success (1701-1714), the republic's leadership chose the losing side and so lost their independence. As a result, Prince Philip was appointed as imperial governor of Mantua in 1714. His rule was mostly benevolent; Philip's main goal was to restore the republic to its former glory as a mecca for artistic and cultural elites. In particular, he wanted his royal court to set a prime example of what Mantua was supposed to be.

Intercourse between Venice and Mantua was frequent and mutually beneficial, even before the war. The change in leadership did little to interrupt the stream of artists and ideas that flowed back and forth between the cities. For Vivaldi, Mantua was his first opportunity to expand his career beyond the confines of his city and immediate region.

Vivaldi's fame had reached the ears of international music lovers and nobles beginning in about 1710, or 1712 at the latest. However, before his appointment to Prince Philip's court, his fame was supported only by word of mouth. He had yet to prove himself on a larger stage. The urge to do just that—prove oneself—may have been one of the leading motivations for Vivaldi to accept the position. Money, of course, was another motivation that couldn't be ignored. Finally, a new position meant a chance to try new things and experiment with new styles, relatively unfettered by the mandates of an institution (the Hospital of Mercy) or the fickle public (San Angelo Theatre). For all these reasons, and probably more, Prince Philips's offer was too good to refuse.

The office of court musical director was taken over by Vivaldi no later than April 1718. By the end of the month, he was opening his first opera in Mantua, *Armida*, at the Arciducale Theatre. The court musical director's full responsibilities were nearly open ended. He had no say in church music, but everything else fell into his lap: music for special occasions, court festivities, opera, commissions for other royals and nobles, and instrumental and vocal music composition for publication, among other duties. Vivaldi oversaw the court orchestra and its 23 members: one director, one organist, nine singers, 2 oboists, four violinists, one violist, one cellist, one contrabass player and three trumpet players. The presence of an actual horn "section" was something slightly new for Vivaldi, and was a stylistic difference between Venetian and Mantuan musical tastes. For many years, historians had a difficult time piecing together exactly what Vivaldi did during his 2-plus years in the court of Prince Philip; recent discoveries of shed more light on his activities.

The prince's ambition was to see Mantua undergo a musical, theatrical renaissance. Years later, in 1735, the Austrian ruling family called Philip back to Vienna due to his generally poor governance—his focus on the finder things meant little time left for the more mundane tasks of leadership. In 1718, he specifically picked Vivaldi to help him enact his grand scheme, and for a while, all worked according to plan.

1719 turned out to be a banner year, not just for Vivaldi, but for the whole Mantuan Republic. Prince Philip was wedded to Princess Eleonora di Guastalla in a lavish ceremony. Vivaldi provided all of the musical accompaniment. He also produced at least four plays for the Arciducale Theatre between 1718 and 1720; he was impresario for some of these, and each achieved healthy profits. In terms of money matters, Vivaldi's compensation as court musical director was far more than he was used to. He officially earned 680 lire each month, several times more than his Pieta salary. At the end of each opera season, he received bonus payments representing the revenue for each production. Although it's not possible to know how much is actually profit, it's fascinating to note that a payment made at the end of the 1720 Carnival totaled 5389 lire.

Experimentation being one of his essential characteristics, Vivaldi tried his hand at a new genre while working in Philip's court. The cantata was a well-established, "courtly" genre that consisted of a vocal part with musical accompaniment. The number of parts and the length of the overall composition were not dictated by any rules. The distinguishing feature of the cantata was that it was usually created with a special occasion in mind, such as a wedding, feast, public holiday, funeral, etc. While in Mantua, Vivaldi wrote nearly 40 cantatas, and he would write several more after leaving the court.

Prince Philip and his court musical director apparently had a strong working relationship. At one point, Vivaldi was permitted to leave the city long enough to assist in the staging of a new opera in Florence. He also had ample work on "the side" to keep him occupied if court duties weren't enough. He worked on commission for elite buyers across Italy and Austria, as well as publishing instrumental and vocal works under his own name. The high esteem in which Vivaldi was held by the Mantuan court partly explains why he was able to eventually leave his post without too much fuss.

In January 1720, the Dowager Empress Eleonora Magdalena passed away; the Austrian Empire entered a period of mourning. Vivaldi used this opportunity to request a leave of absence from Mantua, which Prince Philip immediately granted. According to the terms of their agreement, the prince could recall his court musical director whenever he was needed, but ultimately that never happened. Vivaldi retained his royal title while giving up most of its responsibilities. *La Candace*, launched during Carnival 1720, was the impresario's last opera to be staged as an official member of the Mantuan court.

Vivaldi's relatively brief time in Mantua was transformative in several ways. In the most tangible sense, it gave a significant boost to his personal wealth. It's also possible that he first met the young Anna Giro, who would later become his prima donna, in Mantua. Perhaps most importantly, Vivaldi's royal appointment initiated a period of extensive, even adventurous travels. A decade or more later, he wrote to a friend that he had enjoyed the sights in "many European cities," but, in fact, there's no hard evidence of him traveling beyond Germany. Still, in the 18th century, even a trip across the Alps was no small thing. Vivaldi also forged professional networks with diplomats and aristocrats in Italy, Austria, Bohemia, Germany and the Low Counties. As before, these networks would help him spread his musical influence far and wide.

The period from late 1720 through 1722 is noticeably lacking in terms of biographical material on Vivaldi. His movements and various employments are only hinted at. He was likely traveling a great deal, owing to the fact that he only staged two operas in Venice during the timeframe. In 1722, he may have gone to France to attend the consecration of King Louis XV. Even if he stayed behind, it's likely that he contributed music for the special event. By October of the same year, Vivaldi (and his parents and probably several siblings) moved out of the apartment he had rented for more than ten years, taking new lodgings near the church of Santa Maria Formosa. Renting for 70 ducats a year, these new rooms served the composer until May 1730. His mother died in there in 1728 after a prolonged illness.

After a five-year hiatus, Vivaldi and the Hospital of Mercy came to a new working agreement in 1723. Clearly bowing to their former Master of Violin's new status, the board of governors requested only that he supply the institution with two concertos each month, whether he was in or out of Venice. If he happened to be in Venice, they asked that he make time for at least four rehearsals. The extreme leeway that gave to Vivaldi demonstrates their understanding that, from the impresario's perspective, the Hospital of Mercy was no longer anything except a "secondary" job.

Vivaldi took full advantage of his freedom and leisure; he traveled to Rome, probably for the first time, in 1723. He was so taken with the city that his full creative energy was focused on Roman opera and the Roman nobility for the next two years. His path into the heart of the Roman aristocracy was paved for him with the help of a fellow Venetian musician. Vivaldi entered the "Eternal City" with a letter requesting that Princess Borghese help the impresario make a strong impression and meet the right sort of people. His new Roman connections proved lucrative, as well as beneficial for his career.

By his own accounts, Vivaldi have a private performance in the Pope's chambers and received a strong ovation. More important than the Pope, however, was Cardinal Pietro Ottoboni. The cardinal, being an appreciator of first-rate instrumental music, collected and copied all of Vivaldi's works that he could get his hands on. Dozens of concertos and other arrangements survived only because of the diligence of Ottoboni and his copyists.

After one of his last visits to Rome, in 1725, Vivaldi entered a rewarding relationship with another wealthy patron. He became unofficial court musician for Count Morzin, a Bohemian noble with several enormous estates and palaces. Morzin paid Vivaldi handsomely and seemed to let the Venetian work as a kind of "correspondence" composer. There's convincing evidence that he made at least one trip to Morzin's home, where he conducted the count's personal orchestra. Vivaldi's Opus 8 concertos, published in 1725, contain a dedication to the Bohemian count. Opus 8, with its 12 concertos, is noteworthy for its inclusion of four concertos that together were known as "The Four Seasons."

The Four Seasons

In December 1725, the *Amsterdam Gazette* advertised the publication of Vivaldi's Opus 8. Originally titled "The Test of Harmony and Invention," the collection is one of the finest examples of "program music"—music built around a specific topic or theme. The first four concertos each represented a different season of the year, thus the name "The Four Seasons."

Music critics have said that Vivaldi pushed the envelope of what program music could be with "The Four Seasons." Each concerto was introduced with a sonnet that established the scene for the music. To drive the point home even further, Vivaldi marked specific places in the music that corresponded to lines in the sonnets. The music itself was typically Baroque: inventive, surprising, even somewhat wild. Single, repeated notes and rising/falling scales were used to evoke storms on the horizon. The sounds of birdsong and rippling water were deftly replicated, along with sounds of the hunt, sleep, rain, ice, or simply sitting quietly by a warm fire.

The concertos that made up "The Four Seasons" were likely composed well before their publication. Some may have been written down as early as 1716. In general, program music was not popular in Italy. France and the rest of northern Europe, however, eagerly consumed Vivaldi's imaginative renderings of the natural world.

Chapter 5: Later Life

The period from 1732 to about 1740 was much quieter for Vivaldi than the preceding 20 years. He mostly confined himself to working in Venice, but even here his overall production was down, or at least fewer examples of his work were preserved. Unfortunately for "The Red Priest," fashions had changed in his home city. No longer were his concertos and operas in high demand. He was clearly still recognized and respected, but his fame was on the downward curve.

Vivaldi's changing fortunes became even more evident when he made one of his few trip outside of Venice during the 1830s. Between 1836 and 1839, he made several journeys north of the Alps into Germanic territories. In the past, his name had a way of opening the doors of aristocrats and tastemakers; that was no longer the case. In some cities, he may have been practically anonymous. In 1738, he journeyed to Amsterdam to help celebrate the 100th anniversary of the Schouwberg Theatre. He may have hoped that the excursion would allow him to find new patrons, as Amsterdam was still friendly territory, but the results were disappointing. Increasingly broke and willing to sell his work at even lower prices, he returned to a Venice that was even more unresponsive to his efforts.

Even the opera house, which had always been familiar territory for Vivaldi, was no longer so friendly and safe. For most of the decade, he had no direct ties to any Venetian opera house. His name was not listed as impresario anywhere. It's confirmed that he was still composing at a rapid pace, but his compositions simply didn't attract the same attention. After 1732, he wrote at least 13 operas, a large number given the time frame and the financial worries that were beginning to press on him. After a premier during Carnival in 1734, Vivaldi was absent from the Venetian stage for four years. Not even San Angelo Theatre debuted or revived any of his work during this dry spell.

Vivaldi briefly tried to resurrect his opera career in nearby Ferrara, but the attempt failed miserably. Styles had changed throughout Italy. While Vivaldi's musicianship remained at an extraordinarily high level, audience expectations were entirely different. The work of Johann Adolph Haase dominated opera houses, and his popularity led to a sea of imitators. "Old style" composers, chief among them Vivaldi, were simply pushed out, in favor of the "Neapolitan" style of Haase and his generation. The story has often been repeated in the arts, but it's never any less tragic.

Other than a few modestly successful premiers in Verona at the Filarmonico Theatre, Vivaldi had lost touch with opera audiences. When he did manage to secure backing for a production, it was always in second-rate, less fashionable houses. On several occasions, he had a debut scheduled only to be pre-empted by a revival of a more "modern" work. It must have been extremely frustrating.

For the first time in many years, finances became a serious problem for Vivaldi. It was likely for this reason that he found himself back at the Hospital of Mercy in the hope of once more securing a salaried position. In August 1735, the board of governors voted to hire Vivaldi as Concert Master. The records show that he was paid a salary of 100 ducats a year, which was exactly what he earned when he first entered the hospital 30 years earlier. It was maybe the most telling example of Vivaldi's decline. The yearly salary was a fraction of what the hospital paid him in the 1720s for much less work. Just three years later, he was voted out for the third and final time. His relationship with the hospital didn't end, however; he continued producing work on commission for special events, but his payment for this was slim compared to his glory days. The visit of Saxon prince-elector Frederick Christian was one such special event: in 1740, Vivaldi produced all of the instrumental and vocal music for the festivities, in which the Hospital of Mercy unofficially competed with Venice's other hospitals for the approval of the prince-elector. The royal visit was crucial to Vivaldi scholars for one reason—Christian was an avid music collector, and he safely stored the bound copy of the music presented to him after the festival. He also made a point of acquiring several other Vivaldi collections. These all became part of the Dresden collection, one of the richest sources of original sheet music by the Venetian master.

To supplement his declining income, Vivaldi redoubled his efforts to sell his manuscripts. He deliberately stopped publishing new material, hoping to drive up the price on his existing work. The desperation was obvious, and this strategy only met with limited success. A few of his associates noted in their diaries that Vivaldi was expecting way too much money for his sheet music. Still, he did have noteworthy skill as a businessperson, and he managed to convince a few visiting aristocrats to part with some of their gold and silver.

In 1740, aged 62 years, Antonio Vivaldi chose to relocate one last time, hoping to revitalize his career far from Venice. Before leaving the city, he arranged one final deal with the Hospital of Mercy. The board of governors agreed to purchase a set of concertos and other pieces, but for far less than what Vivaldi had originally hoped. The deal proves that he had no intention of returning. In late May, he received a court summons, but a neighbor reported that he had already left the city. At his age, the bold move across the Alps may have been surprising. However, throughout Vivaldi's life he embraced an independent approach to life. The security of a salaried position was never as appealing as freedom of movement and creativity. The idea of "retirement" probably never entered his mind.

For nearly a year, there are no records of where Vivaldi was or what he was doing. He finally appeared in Vienna in early 1741. Originally, the presence of Emperor Charles VI was the magnet that drew Vivaldi to the Austrian capital. Charles was enthralled by the Venetian's music, even in the twilight of his career. Unfortunately, the emperor died in the fall of 1740. At the same time, the outbreak of the War of Austrian Succession, which lasted until 1748, made Vienna's art and business climate less friendly than usual.

Given the death of his patron, Charles VI, and the skirmishes in the empire, Vivaldi failed to make an impression in Vienna. He tried to strike up a partnership with the Mingotti brothers, Venetian expatriates deeply involved in opera, but the bottom fell out. The troupe was too broke to stage any productions in 1741. Vivaldi tried to cultivate local opera connections, too. He rented a house just one block away from the Kartnertortheater, one of the leading opera venues in the city. The theatre had produced a few Vivaldi operas during the 1730s, but just as in Italy, the Vivaldian style had been replaced.

Vivaldi made a last ditch attempt to parlay his diminished fame into an income stream. He sought an audience with visiting nobleman Anton Ulrich of Thuringia. Twice, Ulrich turned the composer away at his door. On a third occasion, he made time for a brief meeting. It's unknown whether Ulrich ever purchases any manuscripts from the aging Vivaldi. In June 1741, Vivaldi did sell a few compositions to a Count Collato, but the sale price was a fraction of what the Hospital of Mercy had paid him just a year earlier. That he agreed to the minimal compensations shows just how dire his position had become in only a short while.

The last few months in Vienna were no doubt difficult for Vivaldi. He felt abandoned by the musical establishment, unable to produce a new opera and not earning any income from his compositions. In the 1720s, when he had earned enormous sums of money for commissions, and as a court musician, he lived extravagantly. Thus, he saved no money for future hardships. He may not have anticipated the decline in his fame and recognition.

On the 27th or 28th of July 1741, Antonio Vivaldi passed away from an "internal infection." It's possible that his asthmatic condition finally got the best of him. Pneumonia or influenza would have been difficult to overcome with compromised airways. He was buried shortly thereafter in an economical manner at St. Stephen's Cathedral. There was no music at the funeral; the death notices described him as a "secular priest" and made no mention of his renown as a musician and opera impresario. It's likely that his neighbors had no idea that the elderly Venetian once entertained princes, emperors and popes. Both the church where his funeral was held and the home in which he spent his final months were later destroyed.

Chapter 6: Conclusion and Legacy

Other than a few opera revivals in Venice in the 1740s, Antonio Vivaldi's steady decline into obscurity continued after his death. By the end of the Baroque Period (about 1750), his name was unknown and his music almost ignored. Even his most celebrated works, such as "The Four Seasons," were largely forgotten. No other composer of the period underwent such a dramatic rise and fall. His influence, however, was undeniable, even if later generations of musicians couldn't name their source for a particular style or device. Johann Sebastian Bach, in particular, owed a debt of gratitude to Vivaldi for influencing the development of the Baroque and Classical concerto.

Nearly 200 years passed before Vivaldi's reputation was revived. In the early 20th century, several discoveries were made that helped to restore the "Red Priest's" place in music history. In 1926, a boarding school run by an order of monks discovered a collection of original Vivaldi compositions. Not knowing exactly what they were dealing with, the forwarded the collection to the Turin National University Library. Once there, Dr. Alberto Gentili was amazed at what he saw: 97 complete volumes of Vivaldi music. Gentili and the university worked quickly to secure the funds necessary to take possession of the collection. They were lucky to find a willing investor quickly, without tipping off any private collectors of the magnitude of the find.

Once the Turin manuscripts were more closely inspected, it was discovered that they were incomplete. Careful research revealed that any remaining pages were likely in the hands of the descendants of the Durazzo family. Once more, Gentili had to work behind the scenes to reunite the long-forgotten compositions. The Durazzo heir drove a hard bargain, and private funding was once more necessary to secure the additional volumes. Today, the Turin collection of Vivaldi is the richest in the world, with 319 total items. Music scholars from all corners of the globe travel to Turin to see this extraordinary piece of history.

The Turin National University Library, together with composer and pianist Alfredo Casella, organized Vivaldi Week in 1939. The event re-introduced the world to the work of a long-lost Baroque genius. Vivaldi quickly entered the pantheon of greatest composers of not only his own, but any era. Like Back, Mozart and Beethoven, Vivaldi has transcended the academic music establishment and become a composer for the people.

"The Four Seasons" has certainly become Vivaldi's most recognized and often recorded work. The experimental, organic style give the music a timeless quality that is unmatched by anything else from the period. Despite being known mostly as an instrumental composer, Vivaldi produced choral works that have likewise achieved massive popularity. *Gloria* is his most celebrated vocal music and is a staple at Christmas concerts around the world. In total, Vivaldi wrote nearly 500 concertos and possibly almost 100 operas, in addition to countless instructional pieces, vocal pieces, and other arrangements. He was especially known for his ability to compose quickly and on demand.

Vivaldi will probably best be remembered as an innovator and creative genius. He revolutionized both the Italian opera and the concerto form. In fact, he put his own stamp on every musical genre that he touched, from simple arias to concertos with full orchestras. His fame was so immense and his influence so severe, it's surprising that the world forgot him for so long.

Bibliography

"Antonio Vivaldi." (n.d.). Baroque Composers and Musicians.

http://www.baroquemusic.org/bqxvivaldi.html

"Antonio Vivaldi." (2013). Biography.

http://www.biography.com/people/antonio-vivaldi-9519560

"Antonio Vivaldi." (2013). Wikipedia.

http://en.wikipedia.org/wiki/Vivaldi

Heller, Karl. *Antonio Vivaldi: The Red Priest of Venice*. Portland, OR: Amadeus Press, 1997.

Kendall, Alan. *Vivaldi*. London: Elm Tree Books, 1978.

Talbot, Michael. *Vivaldi*. New York: Schirmer Books, 1992.